SHOPS CLOSE TOO EARLY

Shops Close Too Early
© Josh Feit / Cathexis Northwest Press

No part of this book may be reproduced without written permission of the
publisher or author, except in reviews and articles.

First Printing: 2022

Paperback ISBN: 978-1-952869-65-5

Cover Image by Stephanie Browne, New York, NY, stephaniebrowneart.com
Design and Editing by C. M. Tollefson

Cathexis Northwest Press

cathexisnorthwestpress.com

SHOPS CLOSE TOO EARLY
POETRY BY JOSH FEIT

Cathexis Northwest Press

Right back at you, Johnny Rotten Shoes, aka Erica

Table of Contents

Elf Power	19
Athena Dethroned	20
Linger Factor	21
Maybe Metropolis	22
City Planning Pantoum	23
Data Kid Dared Fate	24
Encyclopedia of Heresies	25
A Tanka to Remember Our Ancient City	26
I'm Delighted, My Young Avant-Garde Friend	27
I'm Living My Best Sylvia Plath Life	28
Non-Destination Riders	29
It's Projected to be the Biggest City in the World	30
A Line Around the Block	31
Only in Malady To Discover	32
City Exegesis	33
The Sidewalk is Parallel to the Sky	34
The Sidewalk is Parallel to the Sky	35
A Different Kind of Light Left On, May Sarton	36
The Subway Arts Movement	37
Crush Load	38
What Are the Words to White Man?	40
Shadow Bus	41
On New Year's Eve You Drew a Diagram of the Future	42
Infrastructure	45
Blue Balcony	46
Bus Stop	47
I Didn't Predict Any of This	48
Time at City Spectacles	49
A Food Truck in the Old City	50
Two City Perspectives	51
Sidewalk Plaque	52
You Had Me at Transport, Emily Dickinson	53
Patron of Geography	54
Dwell Time	55
Falsework	56
Evelyn McHale Chooses the Tallest Building in the City	57
Desire Bench	62
To the 7-Eleven	63
The Innisfree Light Rail Extension	64

"He realized he had no idea where he was. He walked until he found a tube station."

—*Hanif Kureishi, Ch. 16, The Black Album*

Elf Power

During a 20th century prom,
Megan and I cut out and saw
the Velvet Monkeys at 9:30 Club.

We were
dressed better than anyone there.

On a smartphone in the next century,
A robot asks me where
I left the bike share.

Listen closely robot: Probably outside the pizza place.

Athena Dethroned

Inevitably, a bildungsroman is a story about the city.
This one updates a myth from the 5th century, B.C.
Remember Athena versus Poseidon—a clash
of Immortals at the Acropolis to see who would become the local deity.

Athena knelt and planted a seed and soon
an olive tree was there, a source of sustenance and light;
industry and rest under its branches.

She became Athena Polias, Goddess of Cities.
For thousands of years, anyway.

Many may not know what the plebeian poets know:
Athena was recently dethroned!

Coming-of-age stories are inevitably
stories about teenagers coming to the city.
At 16, Aldwyn Roberts had a local hit, *Shops Close Too Early*.
He performed it at the district carnival competition and won the top spot—
Calypso King.

He moved to the capital, Port of Spain. He moved to London.
He changed his name to Windrush Generation.

For his clash on Carnaby St.
versus Lady Day and Lady Stardust,
versus Grandmaster Flash and Prince Buster,
versus Beyoncé and Frank "unless a subway is handy" O'Hara,

our Calypso King re-wrote *Shops Close Too Early*
as *The Night of Electric Bikes*.

A handy transubstantiation of time into space.

Athena lovingly transferred her title. After all,
aren't the imperatives of youth just the midnights
of middle age. You pedal past houses
and see through a window, other insomniacs
gathered around a piano's sustenance and light.

Linger Factor

The Department of Transportation sidewalk study ranked my neighborhood 15 points above average. A 24% linger factor.

My neighborhood would score even higher
if the DOT surveyed at night
when youth appear in clinamen lines.

The study found this: People who linger are

    talking to other people, or buying   sandwiches,

                                  using electronics,
    browsing heirloom tomatoes, playing cello,

    waiting for the bus, watching an opera

singer,   giving directions to other people,   exercising,

  brushing someone's hair away from their face,

stretching in the warm 21st century weather,

showing signs of intoxication such as slurred speech or unfocused eyes,

    doing street upkeep like   gardening or sweeping,

asking   for money or food,

    stopping, to take a cellphone picture of jets descending.

If you believe the local columnist,
these neighborhoods where there's evidence of Dvorak's cello harmonics,
ruin everything.

39% of people who linger are reclining,
sitting on benches, for example, or leaning against a wall.
That's what we were doing.

11% of people lingering are reclining on infrastructure not intended for reclining, which indicates need for more infrastructure.

I was leaning on a wall talking to you. Waiting for the bus. Eyes unfocused.
Brushing your hair away from your face.
The linger factor was high.

Maybe Metropolis

Sous les pavés, la plage!

Maybe not! city planner Jane J. says.

Maybe instead,
city poet Frank O. said

(being her political ally,
and always writing about the sun),

the beach
is already
the city.

City Planning Pantoum

The time it takes your lungs to learn Ravi Shankar's midnight raga is the same
as it takes your apartment to turn macadamias into honey. The sweetest story I ever heard was
about the boyfriend who greeted his girlfriend at the station platform dressed in her clothes.
Their future was doomed. The sidewalk is made of broken verse.

The sweetest story I ever heard was about the girlfriend who hung a hammock of stars beneath
the sidewalk canopy for her blind boyfriend. Midnight-to-six
is the metric city planners should use to see the sidewalk. The wind is made of apartment
buildings. Separatist metrics cannot blur the artless notion that shelter is somehow bad for the
neighborhood.

Midnight-to-six is the metric city planners use when they dress in platform shoes to survey the
district. A verse from Bo Diddley's *Pretty Thing* is a rendering of Ravi Shankar's evening.
The artless notion that additional housing is bad, follows the artless notion that shelter requires
mitigation. Apartment buildings are made of our returns from the station.

Greetings, I'm on the art committee for the skate park. The time it takes to turn verses into
resources is the same as to dress in silk. The sidewalk is made of stories about boyfriends &
girlfriends. Like the one about the future, when midnight asks the canopy: Do your lungs have a
favorite song, at this late hour?

Data Kid Dared Fate

Data Kid dared fate,
scheduled a celebration in advance: Made reservations
at a restaurant where you bring your own whiskey.
Such a brazen breach of destiny
that Decima complained to Jupiter:
I'm the one who allots portions around here.

But we went ahead with it:
—a gargoyle poses on a yellow duplex
—a tattoo grows between W Addison and N Pulaski
—the green headlight of a scooter-share scooter
—a field trip into a vanished church.

It's a city because it has imagination.

Immortal Decima be damned,
Data Kid dared fate.
Scheduled a celebration in advance.
Double our portion.
More French fries please.
So brazen, so human.

Encyclopedia of Heresies

Forty thousand people stopped taking the train.
The next day it was 50,000.
Then 60,000. Then 80,000
stopped.

In just a week, an 80% drop
below the baseline before the virus.

It used to be a city

where boyfriends opened
windows at night
to let in cool Sound air.
To let in an Encyclopedia of Heresies.

Like immigration. And
horses galloping in alleys.

But there are no more manifestos
at the Grand St. sandwich shop after shows.

Our blasphemy and bodies are gone.

Our handicrafts,
bridles,
trumpets,
flutes,
jars,
plows,
ships,
and chariots are silent.

Open the window
and what you'll hear is nearness walking away.
The sound of tens of thousands of people
riding an empty train.

A Tanka to Remember Our Ancient City

For a period of seven years, I sang opera arias
floating on water wearing a giant dress made of umbrellas.

I wasn't aware of it at the time.

We were not aware of what we were doing
when we waltzed on
Rte. 355 at 4 AM.
Stepping lightly:
One,
    two,
        three.
        One,
            two,
                three.
We couldn't explain it to the man who swerved
to a halt and emerged
cursing at us from his beige VW Rabbit.

I can explain it now: We saw pavement as a way to tell time.

I'm trying to be more conscious
of what's happening while it's happening.
What are the facts? What are the questions?
What are the options?
And what's it mean?

Let me savor last Friday: The

Siamese cat likes
food wet. Did Sleater-Kinney
release a box set?
We could drive, but let's waltz to
town. Every step cuneiform.

I'm Delighted, My Young Avant-Garde Friend

I'm delighted, my young avant-garde friend,
to know *Sumer is icumen in*.
Let there be light, let there be infrastructure, amen.

New buildings create sky where there's light to bend,
same as spirits once skin.
I'm delighted, my young avant-garde friend.

What's outside isn't pretend.
Heartbreaks. Concussions. The housing supply is thin.
Let there be light, let there be infrastructure, amen.

The photography class is on the sidewalk again,
adventures in light where ceilings have been.
I'm delighted, my young avant-garde friend,

to read what you've written
about what you've seen and haven't seen.
Let there be light, let there be infrastructure, amen.

New buildings create more sky than they apprehend.
Graveyards become parks where ceilings have been.
I'm delighted, my young avant-garde friend.
Let there be light, let there be infrastructure, amen.

I'm Living My Best Sylvia Plath Life

I'm learning piano.
And *Teen Vogue* is publishing my villanelle!

which begins:

Necessity has its very own rules.
Shop the kitchen at the climate crisis.
Wine and garlic will ensure we're consoled,

while bread and legumes will make sure we're full.
Divide the square footage into pieces.
Necessity has its very own rules.

See, just like her, I love the drunk
Welsh poet. Or, just like hers, my heroes are dead.
It's not that I'm learning to play piano,
it's that I'm learning Prince's *Kiss* on piano.

You realize Prince is dead?
my doctor said.

Please do not be alarmed.
I'm living my best Sylvia Plath life.
I want to be Sylvia's best friend.
I want to leave campus with her on Friday afternoon,
sit next to her on the train.
We'll ride into the city. Transfer to the subway.

Necessity has its own rules.

—Subway stations become bomb shelters.

Non-Destination Riders

The first time I rode the subway, Aunt Esther
held my hand because I was scared I'd fall through
the cracks

between cars.

Will tens of thousands of people still ride the subway after the pandemic?
The long-term impacts remain unknown.

There is less eye contact now;
less money spent on booze at Monsoon;
no applause.
We wear more masks, sad they're not part of a rockabilly revival.

The trains have fewer destinations. The days have less form.

The last time I rode the subway, I set my forehead against the consoling glass.
What form

holding hands

will take in the future

remains unknown.

It's Projected to be the Biggest City in the World

All data has its own reason for moving to the city.
Economic sickness

or Sunday family dinner frankfurters with strepitant television.

Seeking opportunity and peace.
Feeling the new amapiano at Sip Lounge.

Fleeing is the same as seeking.

Remember how the Hebrew slaves crossed the Red Sea?

It certainly doesn't have to be that epic.
There was the summer of transferring
trains at Metro Center at midnight
after work, when fleeing and seeking felt like leaping.
The platform replete with improvisation.

Fleeing and seeking are popular
in this age of mental health and scrolling.
History repeats itself. Only faster.

Having just crossed the city under a vellum moon,
the latest seeker falls into a room
of "face-me-I-face-you" housing.
He plugs his electric bike battery into the wall
next to the sequins of cell phone chargers.
The battery light moves toward green,
annulling the day's ride while also confirming it.

Studies project a population of 100 million seekers
and their corresponding lights here.

A Line Around the Block

Lord Kitchener's calypso residency
at 50 Carnaby
elevated him
above Athena: Lord Kitch, the new God of Cities.

This is what happens when your name on the marquee
draws maximum capacity with mixolydian feet.

Just like Athena guided Odysseus
Lord Kitch now guides our city's sackers.

DJ Lace Cadence comes on at 1 am. But fate

once put Cadence on air when Helios was high;
filling in on a Saturday afternoon.

Mischievous DJ.
Incessant patter and lasers.
Explaining to bemused regular listeners
and single-family homeowners:
This is how DJs do it.

"Repurposing sound," he said,
resembling class war, giggling and reassembling,
while graciously addressing
the emails and texts.

I realized something fantastic was afoot,
so I made an offering: I called in a request
Underground Train by Lord Kitchener.

I'm a staffer at the local transit agency.
A devotee of infrastructure. I know building
at least 25 households per acre
reassembles cities to create continuity for bus lines.
Playing music after midnight creates continuity for sightlines.

The city planner and the DJ are both asking the same question:
How do I make this last forever?

Only in Malady To Discover

It's sad when it's time to put away the thermometer.
Only in malady to discover:

the caul of the dishwasher
croon of warm water
along my spine for hours.

Only in malady did I discover,
lifelong phobias become similar.

My fear
of blood draws is like
my fear of the famous night from childhood when
family and friends flew into town on airplanes.
Never had there been such warmth and excitement
in our cigarette ash
and mauve bathrobe home.
Suddenly transformed
by light and conversation.
Food!
The food.
Bread and tapenade. Tomatoes and oil. Shish kebab.
The trays of food.
Me, the Artful Dodger, pocketing
hors d'oeuvre after hors d'oeuvre for hours.

By midnight I was retching
bile on the bathroom floor.
It remains the favorite night of my life.
Never up this late before.

Only in malady to discover,
blood drawn toward possibility.

City Exegesis

3 AM turns cities into earlier centuries.

The streets turn into lanes. Streetlights into lanterns. Faces become countenances. The sky shows up gloomy.

It's 3 AM in Lower Manhattan. The arsonist strolls into the frame wearing tennis shoes, a hoodie, cargo shorts, and a little kid's backpack. His casual countenance reveals his gross misunderstanding of the facts. Sure, 3 AM lends itself to dreamy yearnings. But this is no time to downplay reverie. A serious enterprise: The songs we believe in after midnight are synonymous with the year I spent trapped in an apartment among living and dead mice, didn't bathe once, and arrived two hours early to a party I was barely invited to with cuts all over my face from the disposable razor. But don't ever forget this either: Years later, in the dining car of the Coast Starlight, I took the porter's advice and leaned out the door of the moving train to celebrate the blue and orange wind.

The arsonist crosses mid-block, carrying a Bic lighter, looking like he needs a shower, and believing in the Old Testament's politics of fire. The footage catches him in the act. He walks toward the outdoor dining canopy in front of Prince St. Pizza, holds the lighter to it, flips back his biblical hair, and then strolls away as a bush of flames grins for the camera. The incriminating video startled the city and helped the police tie him to at least one other felony arson two blocks away where another outdoor dining tent had burned down.

It turns out, this arsonist was none other than *Food & Wine's* recent Sommelier of the Year. Once the wine director at Eleven Madison Park, the best restaurant in the world, according to the *New York Times*. And currently, at 35, the managing partner at La Compagnie des Vins Surnaturels, his own successful Soho bar. You'd think curating cups of wine would make him an ally to the city's singers, belly-dancers, sorcerers, workers, jesters, shop owners, smooth-skinned lads, and spies. These outdoor dining tents that have replaced parking spaces worldwide are theirs. Restaurants at night that turn into parks during the day; that turn into vaccine clinics, pop-up clothing shops. Dining cars on trains.

The sommelier's crime insinuates more than arson. I'd charge him with ignoring this century's yearnings. I want to sit him down and tell him: The city is not against you. The night is for you. For you, who

doesn't want to know. For you, who
doesn't even know what's happening. For you, who

wants to know, but is too shy to ask. Drink your four cups of wine, children.
From here on out, the Old Testament doesn't have to be the sole domain of pyromaniacs.

The Sidewalk is Parallel to the Sky

On an afternoon of errands,
parallel is what?

Sidewalks run parallel to streets,
but also perpendicular to streets.

The prescription at Walgreens runs parallel
to the narrative of your body, but perpendicular to your fate.

As evening sets in, buildings rise parallel to buildings,
but at right angles to dancing

where modes zigzag. I swerve block by block home
where it's safe to weep about Mom's childhood friend.

To Mom's bewilderment,
Bev stopped calling a few weeks ago.

I tracked her to a hospital phone number in New Jersey.
She sounded drugged and resigned.

I told her Mom missed their weekly calls.
Bev hedged her fate, and said she would try to call Mom soon.

Now, for the first time in 80 years,
Mom is the only one who remembers the walk home

from Jefferson High School.
West along New Lots. South on Malta.

Perhaps, if they were feeling rowdy, they would walk east
on Pitkin Ave. to catch the C Train to Rockaway Beach for a swim.

Today, Mom got lost in the suburbs walking to the pool.
We eventually found her weeping.

Bev may have been there too.
Because the sidewalk is.

The Sidewalk is Parallel to the Sky

because when you're living in a city

— parallel is what?

Sidewalks run parallel to streets,
but they also run perpendicular
to streets.

They cross intersections.
They love the park
and move versus cars.
Sidewalks zigzag to Shaula Doyle's apartment.
and descend to the waterfront.

Remember this though: The sidewalk is only
—and always—
parallel to the sky.

Orient yourself.

Light rail travels parallel to future polling places.
The port reclines adjacent to the world.
Students share rooms oblique to world history.
Buildings rise next to buildings at right angles to nightclubs,
with piano chords stirring.

Music is written parallel to invocations.

Billie Holiday stands in the hallway, extending her arms
—parallel to what?

Remember: When you're living in a city, you're conducting a seance.

A Different Kind of Light Left On, May Sarton

When I walk into the apartment,
the music's already on,
a frequent
phenomenon.

                        A different kind of light
left on, May Sarton.
I planned it this way.
House plants tended to

                        by Billy Strayhorn.
The walls wondering
what's alive in here

                        while I was gone,
to Walgreens.
I come waltzing in,
the walls singing
A Flower is a Lovesome Thing,
using the chromatic scale Strayhorn imagined in.
PAR can light still on
him.
I've given you the key to my apartment
where you discover disembodiment.

It couldn't have been easy,
ghostwriting

                        while I was gone.

The Subway Arts Movement

In the public Department of Transit
meeting room
your smile
is a bore

my headphone
cord

is more

mischievous.

A white braid
of graffiti

across

agency furniture.

The trainyard tag says:
"You're Whispering."

So, it's true. You can hear me.

Crush Load

During rush hour,
subway ridership can hit 200%
capacity. City
planners call it Crush Load.
14-16 people standing per one square meter.

The official limit is 6 people
per one square meter,
before all the square meters turn into details
from *Fall of the Damned into Hell*.

Crush Load can turn tragic
in a suicidal city
like Tokyo.
A despondent commuter jumps in front of a subway train
at least once a day.

City planners are trying to address the epidemic.
They've installed blue LED lighting in the stations.

They've commissioned a video game composer, a former electronic musician, to write calming songs.

These "train departure melodies" serenade the public as they wait.

Tokyo's English-language paper reports:

Each jingle is a story, the composer said,
sitting between instruments and computer screens.
"The journey from Shibuya to the next station is a very steep slope."

The rapturous crescendo and rising pitch in Shibuya's departure song
is about the train's uphill journey to the next platform.

There are no departure songs in Seattle's stations.
Just quinoa in my pocket, and I don't know what to do with it.

Nor are Seattle's suicide numbers remarkable.
They're below the county and the state,
and far below Tokyo's morbid rate.

(Why does everybody think the place they live commits the most suicide?)

And Seattle doesn't even come close to hitting Crush Load.

Such a boring city.

Or is it?

We are the rare American city
where transit ridership is actually increasing
No. 1 in that social justice category!
with 224 million daily boardings, Seattle Transit Blog writes.

And from personal research, I can say our Crush Load is
high.

Crushing it at
the Jefferson St. basketball court.

Crushing millet, blueberries, and ice.

You've got
secret crushes,
and fleeting crushes.

Verboten crushes.
Your crushes on the #41.
Timeless crushes.
You & me
on the plane to Ataturk in Istanbul,
or National in DC.
You crush my hand in your hand.
Your pistachio mouth,
drinking from the Bosphorus,
which, despite our departure, still exists.

The crush to end all crushes.

We're the only two in the station.
Under blue LED trees.

And maybe
the composer writes a song for us.
A departure melody,
all uphill.

What Are the Words to White Man?

I remember a little boy, perhaps Jewish,
perhaps born in Ankara,
oohing and ahhing over his mother's makeup and asking
if he can put some on
too. When she says he can he does.
As he does he whispers: "Becoming beautiful."

30 years later, I saw him, now a Marxist guitarist,

signing autographs on Broadway.
I called out: What are the words to *White Man in Hammersmith Palais?*

He came over to tell me everything
he was able to

remember.

Long after that, waiting on the sidewalk, I asked myself
is that really her coming over in the Marxist dress?
She kissed me.

The news said
they played *White Man*
at his funeral.
Perhaps I'm becoming beautiful.

Shadow Bus

After-hour rush hour is
the subconscious of economics.
Remember Pirate Jenny
counting the wondering heads
while she's cleaning ratty beds.

Metro is not good at planning for the subconscious.
They always seem to need
to send a second bus late at night.
They call it a Shadow Bus.

Ladies and gentlemen. It's two o'clock in the morning. There's a full moon out.
The forest faeries are riding Citi Bike. There's no affordable housing.
I'm on Percocet in the park! The light casts my shadow on the basketball court.

On New Year's Eve You Drew a Diagram of the Future

On New Year's Eve you drew a diagram of the USB and the computer:
connect the laptop to the TV
and the microphone to the mixer;
run the headphones through the jack-splitter
necessary for karaoke. Apartments of the world unite.

You drew yourself into the diagram,
a stick figure singing.

I think a diagram is a crystal ball.

As with all futures, your figure
will eventually disperse. Come apart
like a game of hangman in reverse.

January and the shower curtain

is in the background during your conference call on the bathroom floor.
A smile on your lips announces your fondness of the afterlife.
That's my boyfriend's Creature from the Black Lagoon shower curtain,
you explain to your colleagues.

I bought it when we first got together.
I must have been imagining a midnight double feature.

February and the living room rug

is an Amtrak roomette
on an imagined cross country visit
to our families.

March and the weather

must be nicer
because now you're sitting in the bedroom looking out the window,
watching the hummingbirds you invited over
for lunch: One cup of water to every quarter cup of sugar.
Boil the water with the sugar, make sure it dissolves.

Maybe you're talking in your sleep because you ate all those poppy seeds.
What you said was:
Tomorrow, I will
re-do my will
and sign up for that thing where I am composted.

More visions of coming apart.
Place the body in a steel vessel and lay it on a bed of alfalfa,
wood chips, and straw. Keep it at 131 degrees.
After 72 hours, it will disintegrate and yield a cubic meter of soil.

They're quoting your Buddhism on the state senate floor.
You're a mirror in front of the trees. You look gorgeous in that green
jacket, Girl.

April and the backyard cottage

is in the nearby forest.
A Saturday night drive through island roads.
You explain: *While driving a car, I inadvertently follow my bike routes.*

We get our first dose of the vaccine in Jason's sister's kitchen.

We think we've marked the end of the pandemic by
finding a punch bowl at the Goodwill,
the only place punch bowls exist.

Arrange the fruit in a 5-cup ring mold; add 3/4 cup of water;
freeze until solid. Combine the lemonade, limeade, and orange concentrate
over the ice; add 2 cups of water and ginger ale until spumy.
The ice melts slowly.

May and our 2nd shots

at 10:30 AM in the rec center tents.
Like potato peels fermenting, can you smell if it's working?

June and we do

visit our families.
Take Metro from Union Station to the Pentagon
to Bus Bay L3 and then the #29
to a stop one block from your childhood home
and your mom's backyard hummingbird sanctuary.

At 4 AM, I grab my phone in the dark so I can record the rain
beading on the skylight.

The game of hangman is ending now.

July and we

follow your bike route
to the forest where you hung 1,000 paper birds.

Will they still be there?

You're in the diagram. And then you're not.

Infrastructure

The head understands
bodies create more space than
they eliminate.
The exact same math defines
the souls of elevators.

Blue Balcony

In the shower, the blue plastic mat is a balcony.
Look at the city.
I can see where they're building the new light rail station.
I hope everyone can see.

Certainly, not everyone is able to stand drunk in an apartment
and sing a perfect rendition
of Elvis Presley's
Heartbreak Hotel.

The cell phone rings.

"Elvis Presley here."
*"Hello, Elvis Presley. This is Molly Ivins with the New York Times.
I'm calling to write your obituary."*

In the shower, the blue plastic mat is a balcony.
I hope everyone can see.

Bus Stop

I thought the Metro bus was coming.
I saw its LED display
a few blocks away.
But there it stayed, twinkling.

Maybe it wasn't a bus.
Maybe it was just the season's more luminous leaves.

This would have been
the third optical illusion today.

A demon turned out to be a neighbor's picnic umbrella.
A centaur was really you wearing only my shirt.

Unlike illusions, days are kinetic.
No more waiting.
Lights approaching.
The #8 emerging from leaves.

I Didn't Predict Any of This

I predicted I'd be depressed over the holiday weekend.
But surprises undo omens.

Dad, you were brilliant. And the whiskey you served was tasty.
And it was perfect, the DC bureau chief and me
editing the suburbs in a coffee shop next to Safeway.

I was happy spending money too, on a pro basketball ticket,
knowing the Metro is a manifesto,
and the escalator leading into mixed use footsteps is a mystery train.

My exurban niece, cozy in her teenage constellation,
including one boy among the young stars, whose purple non-binary fingernails
were philosophically draped over her shoulders.

Perhaps the biggest surprise of all: A nighttime text from a woman who,
I kid you not, bears a hilarious resemblance to ————. Hush.

And Dad, I seriously love this legit art film. This time capsule starring pretty hippie kids
converging with standing ovations
for Ravi Shankar for God's sake.

Luck comes to me: I didn't expect we'd be loving a movie together again. This late. You 87,
going on 88.

It's true, good luck comes to those who plan. But surprises come to those
who run it back—win by two, threes are twos, call your own foul, ball in.

I'm never 100 percent happy, because I know there's always a doctor's appointment
with the blood work chart looming.
The violent LabCorp techs say, "Is A Girl Named Bill Russell still your emergency contact?"
And then, "We have to do it over! Let's get it over with! He's got a big vein over there!"

I didn't realize: There was a job available writing about transit-oriented development.

And I didn't think: My old friend Wendy's Stealing Clothes would actually be part
of our great neighborhood coup. But she was. Smart AF, her Judah-the-Maccabee-as-fuck
sweater was an amicus brief. I can't believe it:
Even with my mentally ill left arm smarting, my lab chart was all good.

I'm still swooning over the verisimilitude of the groovy art movie,
this late with us.

As it turns out: We can chart the immeasurable.

Time at City Spectacles

I've added *Come on Eileen* to the piano set. It's the only song not prescribed by
the *Real Book* standards. I'm not an apostate, but I'm not a fascist either.
I realize beliefs are just favorite lines of poetry.

I've added *Message to You Rudy*, also not prescribed. I'm not an apostate, but

I got off the subway one stop early. The Wholesome Basket is there at the corner
of Graham & Metropolitan. They have my favorite sandwich.

Friday night. Summer in Brooklyn. I walk the rest of the way to the Airbnb,
clutching my dinner wrapped in paper
and carrying a duffel bag of clothes and lisinopril.

The young host brings me up to date on the 2021 Iranian election. His parents are from Tehran.
The 1979 revolution is not important to him. I stand in the kitchen savoring my meal.
Oh my God, the sublime air conditioner!
A metal pail on the window sill collects every drop.

I have two luminous vodkas at the nearby bar. I drink on the roof-top deck looking east,
past the fence of light bulbs and four-story buildings that create more sky above
the expressway. Youths there, believing in drugs.
They believe in Big Science printed on my shirt.

A tipsy person on the sidewalk wants to know where they can plug in their Juul.

I wait outside the Airbnb for Fay Wray and Gregor Samsa.
They are driving up from Virginia.
My legs are dangling over the railing.

Our hosts are high. They've been smoking pot on the back porch.
There's lime-green slush in the ice tray. Their friend is crashed
in dishabille on the couch.

Please add Donna Summer's *I Feel Love* to the *Real Book*. What can I say?
I think the bios in the back of poetry journals are more exciting than the poetry. It's like how the
apartments in the backgrounds are more interesting than the porn.

A Food Truck in the Old City

The wrong street design sets traps
decades to come. Star-crossed lovers already knew this.
Peacemakers too.
Is there no way to save the Old City? Is there some burnt offering?

An economics professor and an environmental science professor at
UCLA
used satellite images and data from Google Maps to reveal these traps
to the rest of us.

Their study of 29 million miles
found 10.8 million dead-ends worldwide.
A surfeit of cul-de-sacs paralyzing the houses and buses.

I know no one around here. Shops close too early.
No six-plexes nor kisses.

Their abstract concluded:
Today's choices for street connectivity may
lock us into tragic pathways.

But perhaps some good luck!
Another study found the opposite of dead-ends
are food trucks.
Bushwhack the tragic cul-de-sacs.

I still have to submit my study for peer review.
Thankfully, last night's shish kebab cinders
revealed who my peers may be.

Two City Perspectives

To your place or mine:
waterfront workers in cranes,
birds in maple trees.

Sidewalk Plaque

The #2 bus pulled up to Sunset & Crescent Heights.
Google Maps said I'd arrived. *The destination is on your right.*

Sightseeing in L.A. I'd arrived at a Chase Bank, a drive-through branch, fronting a strip mall parking lot. But the afternoon's real destination was the adjacent traffic island.

No address there and bare,
but where once Love,
Sloths,
Seeds
played a place called Pandora's Box.
(City Hall had worried Pandora's myth was coming true on Sunset Strip. The kids were hopeful about this too.)

Their curfew riot was one of many Constitutional amendments that year.
Pauli & Betty starting NOW. Stokely saying "Power." The riot at Compton's Cafeteria.

Compton's Cafeteria no longer exists, but at least there's a plaque on the sidewalk.

Compton's
Cafeteria Riot 1966

Here marks the site of
Compton's Cafeteria where a riot
took place one August night when
transgender women and gay men
stood up for their rights and fought
against police brutality, poverty,
oppression and discrimination
in the Tenderloin

There's no plaque at the barren traffic island on Sunset Strip.
Allow me:

Pandora's Box
Curfew Riot 1966

Here marks the site
                   where
                   night
stood up.

You have arrived. Your destination is found in others.

You Had Me at Transport, Emily Dickinson

O! Make me a personal mass transit map—

Martian Jenny Place
Student Nonviolent Coordinating Committee Square.
Falafel Paper Park.

But what shall I call the hub—
at the heart of the city

where my spirit is the numerator divided
by east, west, south, and northbound trains?

O, I know!
Friday Night Station.

Bread & wine –
at the center of time &

throe.

Patron of Geography

Your roommate decided. He's leaving the city and moving
to the suburbs, back to his childhood home.
His parents are moving into a nearby facility. He's given up on art.

There will be no more exasperating the world's police state
with smoke and flowers.
He's taken a job as an administrative assistant at his old high school.
He told you this as you drifted off to TV, one hand on your next glass of wine,
the other on your open-heart surgery.

You're thinking: *He always got such rave reviews.*
You're thinking: *This will be his first paycheck and health care.*

You're thinking: *Can I be alone?*

Do you have the right to ask these questions?
No. While you've always been his patron,
paying for food and rent, you've never commissioned anything. Who has
given up on art now?

Not the regional transit agency, our patron of geography.
They are awarding $100 million for local station access projects.
The evaluation criteria were connectivity, safety, utility, and fertility.
The agency rated applicants "Highly Recommended," "Recommended,"
or "Not Recommended."

I don't work in station access, but having kept *A Thief's Journal*
for one 365-day weekend in Paris, I know these proposals need to be part of a larger plan.

The agency rated one suburb "Highly Recommended" for allowing 25-story buildings.
Imagine luminescent bridges and sky-garden connectivity at North 325th St.
Not so my failed city. It got "Not Recommended"
because the land near the future stations was designated Low-Rise,
the quietest up-zone. Imagine our favorite shop without music.

I imagine your beneficiary evaluated his escape with metrics of his own.
So Ken, is there a larger plan?

Circle one:
A. Highly Recommended
B. Recommended
C. Not recommended

to have one's favorite artist living in the suburbs.

Dwell Time

Metro planners are trying to decrease dwell time,
the amount of time the bus or the train, the north bound equinox, waits at the stop.

There are policy tricks.

All-door boarding,
Off-board payment,
Digital accounts.

There are infrastructure tricks.

Dedicated right of way, queue jumps,
inline stops, so buses don't have to pull in and out of traffic.

And center platforms, so passengers—spies, alcoholics, employees, jesters, extortionists, belly dancers, smooth-skinned lads—can board and exit trains on opposite sides.

We're all trying to reduce the time we spend dwelling.

There are tricks for this too.
Learning Smokey Robinson's three against four.
DMing her mystical final scene.

But, I should tell you—singers, quacks, sorcerers, night walkers—
these are only infrastructure fixes.

There are no policy solutions for this condition.

And I should tell her,
if we're smoking pot, we're not sober.

Nor are you Cesar Chavez.
You are 1,871 miles away,
And this app sucks.

Falsework

Before the work crews
build a bridge to carry light

rail over I-5,
they must first
build the falsework
that will hold the job in place.

When it falls away,
behold.

But until then
be held

by falsework.

Don't today's trusses—
a shower,
a drink, a tune on the piano—
carry us?

Evelyn McHale Chooses the Tallest Building in the City

Anhedonic Evelyn McHale lit her WAC uniform on fire.
Her smile looked like a Brooklyn accent.

Her fiancé, Lt. Barry Rhodes, didn't know about pyromancy. So,
when Evelyn burned her bridesmaid's dress after his brother's wedding

—"I never want to see it again," Evelyn said,
as she performed an impromptu exorcism in the basement—

Barry didn't recognize this, nor think anything more
than what he would later tell the newspapers. "She was afraid

she wasn't good enough for me. I thought I talked her out of that,"
he said with his wry Spencer Tracy smile.

Evelyn often told Barry he looked like a young Spencer Tracy,
daydreaming that she herself was Hollywood's Jeanette MacDonald.

They met at a New Year's Eve house party on Long Island.
Barry grew up on the pretty side of Atlantic Ave., a block from the bay.

Now, he was studying on the G.I. bill a few hours west of Manhattan.
Evelyn was as a bookkeeper on Pearl St. in the Financial District.

Evelyn was living at her brother's on the not-pretty-side of Atlantic.
There's a photo of her standing in the backyard.

In that picture, as opposed to the famous one,
Evelyn's shoes are on, her eyes are open.

Evelyn McHale was not a nebulous youth
like Bennington art student Paula Weldon,

a vegetarian imagining
the sweet, sharp sensation of being burned alive.

With the exception of the WAC fire,
Evelyn wasn't interested in watercolors.

The police report said Paula "disappeared from the face of the earth"
after she "walked into the woods."

That's what Evelyn McHale wanted when she left Barry's abruptly
on May 1, 1947 for the soft train ride of dreams back to the city.

She arrived at Penn Station at 9 AM. Instead of continuing
on to Pearl St., she went up to the street and walked one block

to the southeast side of 31st and 7th and entered
the brass-tinted lobby of the Hotel Governor Clinton.

The next hour is a mystery.
Did Evelyn find an alcove in the mezzanine,

where a stately settee under starfish chandeliers
became her apse and altar?

Did she summon her childhood medium, a girl she called Margaret Smith,
for morning tea? We don't know.

Which gives us an opportunity to cross the East River,
and go to Queens, to the UN at Flushing Meadow,

where the Egyptian ambassador
has been speaking in riddles.

———"I am prepared not to insist on a vote at this time," Mahmoud Hassan Pasha said,
but "I will not withdraw my proposal."

The General Committee remained
bewildered, adjourning

at 12:03 in the morning, May 1, 1947.
Hassan Pasha was becoming non-aligned.

The UN reconvened at 10 AM. With just cause, Hassan Pasha reintroduced his proposal.
The termination of the mandate over Palestine. The declaration of independence.

The UN President said it couldn't be voted on
because it no longer existed.———

The UN is not wholly unrelated to Evelyn McHale.
At that very moment, a UN chauffeur ferried a dignitary to or from

the Empire State Building, and parked the black Cadillac,
pretty as a mausoleum, on W 34th St.

The chauffeur knew a drug store coffee counter
nearby, thereby he was free.

A few blocks southwest, on 31st and 7th Ave.,
Evelyn started her walk into the woods

along the bright mineral sidewalks,
alongside the nervous systems of other people.

Wearing a white scarf and a gray cloth coat,
pearls, gloves, and her favorite shoes, she didn't have far to go.

East on 31st, north on 6th, east on 34th,
into the Art Deco lobby of the Empire State Building.

She purchased a ticket for $3.58, crossed the terrazzo floor
and took the elevator to the observation deck on 86.

She folded her coat over the granite parapet, placed her purse
and makeup kit next to it, and leapt from the tallest building in the world.

Patrolman John Morrissey, working the intersection below,
noticed a white scarf swirling near the upper floors.

Before Morrissey had time to process this,
he heard a crash of glass and staved metal.

Blessed by the wind, Evelyn had
cleared the Empire State Building's geometry.

Unlike the scarf, she fell —122 miles per hour,
20 stories per second—1,050 feet to her death on W 34 St.

She landed like a depth charge into the roof of a UN limousine,
warping its steel frame and shattering its windows.

A young man named Robert Wiles was across the street
with his Graflex camera.

He saw Evelyn, eyes closed and enlightened
in pearls and wreckage, white gloves and bare feet:

Greta Garbo as *The Death of Marat*.
10:44 AM, May 1, 1947.

Wiles ran over and snapped a photo of her lifeless body
The Picture of the Week in the next issue of *Life*.

Men in their Midtown hats clotted around the detonated limousine,
in disbelief at the concurrence of violence and grace.

Detective Frank Murray from the W 30th Precinct
raced upstairs and surveyed the 360° brick sky deck.

He saw where Evelyn had neatly left the contents of her life
nestled on the ledge above the city.

The purse contained several dollars,
The makeup compact was stuffed with family photos.

Evelyn's father was a banker. Evelyn's mother left the family
when Evelyn was in high school.

Evelyn had six siblings. They all called Evelyn *Ebby*.
Evelyn Francis McHale was born September 20th, 1923 in Berkeley, CA

to Vincent Richard McHale of St. Louis, MO,
and Helen Constance McHale, née Smith, of Little Rock, AR,

daughter of Margaret Smith, whom Ebby may have tried to contact
in the lobby of the Hotel Governor Clinton.

Vincent got a Wall Street job and settled the family
in a wealthy Westchester suburb along the Hudson North Line

where parties turned out to be slurred hands in the kitchen,
while clusters of strangers sang *Stardust* around the piano.

Evelyn's mother Helen remained upstairs in her mauve bathrobe.
In her hallways. And Ebby wanted to be Jeanette MacDonald.

Impenitent Paula Weldon, wanted
to see the abandoned amusement park by the lake.

Daydreaming she was the Page of Wands,
Paula took the city bus as far as it would go.

In 1940, Vincent and Helen divorced. Vincent got custody
and Evelyn moved with him to St. Louis where she finished

high school. The Normandy High yearbook said, *While quiet,*
Evelyn was an intelligent conversationalist on any subject.

After graduation, Evelyn got a job as an Office Machine Operator
in the Women's Army Corps. When she was discharged,

she burned her uniform, sneaking the blue kerosene can
off base to a copse of willows next to the Mississippi River.

If Lt. Rhodes had walked into the kitchen
five minutes earlier on New Year's Eve 1945 into 1946,

he would have heard Evelyn McHale making claims of divination
to a neighborhood girl home on break from Bennington.

Paula Weldon took the bus past where butchers sell meat,
but didn't find the amusement park.

Detective Murray found the note in Evelyn's pocketbook, scrawled
on butterscotch embossed stationary from the Hotel Governor Clinton.

Tell my father, I have too many of my mother's tendencies.
My fiancé asked me to marry him in June. He is much better off without me.

I don't want anyone in or out of my family to see any part of me.
Could you destroy my body by cremation?

The New York Times ran a brief item on pg. 23:
Empire State Leap/Ends Life of Girl, 20.

Evelyn Francis McHale, who leaped from the 86th floor,
was cremated, according to her wish.

The limo driver got the day off, which,
he complained to his wife, was wholly unnecessary.

Nonetheless, the couple took advantage of the unforeseen
holiday by going for a pleasure drive

along the Queensboro Bridge into Manhattan
with their scarves swirling.

Desire Bench

Johnny Rotten Shoes and me,
the best metro planners there be.

We came across a discarded futon frame,
And left it at the #48.

Reframe your city
Reclaim your infrastructure:

The apartment building walk-up railings look like symphony harps.

Pedestrian signs don't need words, just keyboard flats and sharps.

In her book, NYC's DOT Director explained desire lines like this:
"The spontaneous way people use public spaces, often contradicting the way the space
was designed. These signatures are usually direct, practical, and leave physical evidence behind."

If you're waiting for the #48,
but you don't want to stand,
our futon frame is still there
for your weight—
and per public demand.

To the 7-Eleven

With the megacity laid out before us,
it's a good idea to stop here.

Bask in its goodwill of honey
mustard pretzel pieces and spotted bananas
because after tonight's scotch,
the walk home from our illuminated port
will end: You in the kitchen,
foraging for snacks.
I have none.

Our neighborhood is now
a camera full of ferries.

The Innisfree Light Rail Extension

Cutting life by 75 percent could prevent death. It also means an 80 percent drop in people riding light rail. It means more time for reading a 1,000-page book of Irish poems. That book

is about destinations. Will they still build light rail extensions to Federal Way and Lynnwood. Will there be a spirit ship

to Byzantium?

When life starts again,
will we travel by magic?

For example, pick a poem, any poem.

"Elf Power" appeared in Spillway;
"Linger Factor" appeared in Vallum;
"City Planning Pantoum" appeared in High Shelf;
"A Tanka to Remember" appeared in Novus Literary
Arts Review;
"Encyclopedia of Heresies" appeared in CircleShow;
"I'm Delighted, My Young Avant-Garde Friend," appeared in
Cathexis Northwest Press;
"City Exegesis" appeared in Novus Literary Arts Review;
an early version of "The Sidewalk is Parallel to the Sky"
appeared in High Shelf;
"What are the Words to White Man?" appeared in
The Halcyone Literary Review;
"Infrastructure" appeared in Novus Literary Arts Review;
"Blue Balcony" appeared in Bee House;
"Bus Stop" appeared in Not a Press;
"I Didn't Predict Any of This" appeared in
The Halcyone Literary Review;
"You Had Me at Transport, Emily Dickinson" appeared in
An Evening with Emily Dickinson from Wingless Dreamer;
"Desire Bench" appeared in Not A Press.

Parts of "Linger Factor" use language from the City of Seattle's
Department of Transportation 2018 public life study.

The first two lines of "A Tanka to Remember Our Ancient City" quote
the "About" page on Dutch composer Laura Stavinoha's website.

In "Evelyn McHale Chooses the Tallest Building in the City," the
headline to the New York Times' May 2, 1947 pg. 23 story about
McHale's suicide—"Empire State Leap/Ends Life of Girl, 20,"—
misstated her age. Evelyn McHale was 23.

Josh Feit is a longtime Seattle journalist. He co-founded the independent Seattle news site PubliCola, where he reported on state and city policy for nearly a decade. Prior to that, Feit was the news editor at Seattle's alternative weekly, the Stranger. More recently, Feit has worked as a speechwriter; first for the Seattle Mayor's Office and currently for Sound Transit, Seattle's regional transit agency. He continues to write a city planning column for PubliCola.

Feit's poetry has been published in Spillway, Vallum, the Halcyone Literary Review, and CircleShow, among other journals. He was a finalist for the 2021 Wolfson Chapbook Poetry Prize and the 2019 Lily Poetry Prize. He won Honorable Mention in Vallum's 2020 Award for Poetry. This is his first published collection, and he has a chapbook forthcoming from Finishing Line Press. He lives in Seattle's Capitol Hill neighborhood, which has some of the deepest tree canopy in the city, alongside some of Seattle's densest housing. You have it backwards, NIMBYs.

Also Available from Cathexis Northwest Press:

<u>Something To Cry About</u>
by Robert Krantz

<u>Suburban Hermeneutics</u>
by Ian Cappelli

<u>God's Love Is Very Busy</u>
by David Seung

<u>that one time we were almost people</u>
by Christian Czaniecki

<u>Fever Dream/Take Heart</u>
by Valyntina Grenier

<u>The Book of Night & Waking</u>
by Clif Mason

<u>Dead Birds of New Zealand</u>
by Christian Czaniecki

<u>The Weathering of Igneous Rockforms in High-Altitude Riparian Environments</u>
by John Belk

<u>If A Fish</u>
by George Burns

<u>How to Draw a Blank</u>
by Collin Van Son

<u>En Route</u>
by Jesse Wolfe

<u>sky bright psalms</u>
by Temple Cone

<u>Moonbird</u>
by Henry G. Stanton

<u>southern athiest. oh, honey</u>
by d. e. fulford

<u>Bruises, Birthmarks & Other Calamities</u>
by Nadine Klassen

<u>Wanted: Comedy, Addicts</u>
by AR Dugan

<u>They Curve Like Snakes</u>
by David Alexander McFarland

<u>the catalog of daily fears</u>
by Beth Dufford

<u>Vanity Unfair and Other Poems</u>
by Robert Eugene Rubino

<u>Destructive Heresies</u>
by Milo E. Gorgevska

<u>Bodies of Separation</u>
by Chim Sher Ting

Cathexis Northwest Press